The Spaces of Labour travelling exhibition ran at
The Lighthouse, Scotland's Centre for Architecture,
Glasgow, from 14 November 2009 to 14 March 2010.

CONTENTS

FOREWORD

Arriving as it does, during a time of adverse global economic conditions, the Spaces of Labour exhibition, which explores relationships between people, culture, places and the economy, could hardly be more fitting. It acts to remind us of how swiftly global and national economic pressures and frameworks can change, and highlights the dramatic impact these changes can have on our communities as well as our urban and rural landscapes. The current financial climate does, however, provide a timely opportunity to explore the way in which new economic opportunities can be exploited, as well as considering afresh the relationship between traditional and new industries and how this can be linked to specific architectural proposals. In a time of a global economic downturn, it is particularly interesting to see this exhibition speculate on where the new economic opportunities might lie.

This exhibition also highlights the often neglected cultural value in our now lost and irreplaceable industrial heritage and it is a reminder that we need to take greater care with what remains. For example, the mapping of the 200 harbours on Scotland's east coast builds on a previous Lighthouse exhibition on the Scottish coastline (6,000 miles) and provides scope for a debate about how our maritime culture could be revived. The students' approaches have ranged from broad strategic propositions to detailed examinations of how specific industries could be developed. The work on display also demonstrates how mapping

and documentation of important areas of our built heritage can act as a stimulus for new thinking and new approaches to development which go beyond more immediate short term concerns about getting the economy back into growth. The exhibition demonstrates the value of a carefully considered and creative approach to anticipating and accommodating change in built and natural environment of Scotland.

The Scottish Government's vision is that "*economic development should raise the quality of life of the Scottish people through increasing economic opportunities for all, on a socially and environmentally sustainable basis*". The postgraduate students at Strathclyde University's Department of Architecture deserve great credit for the scope and breadth of the beautifully presented ideas on show in this exhibition which directly respond to issues raised by the Government's stated vision for Scotland. If we wish to see sustainable development in its widest sense in our cities, towns and rural areas then stronger links between cultural history and spatial planning must be forged and we need to fully recognise the cultural and social value also contained in so many diverse aspects of our built heritage.

Ian Gilzean
Chief Architect
Scottish Government

LANDSCAPES OF PRODUCTION

On the Origins of Spaces of Labour

S.O.L like its predecessor G.L.A.S, (Glasgow Letters on Architecture and Space), emerged out of a postgraduate design studio at Strathclyde University's Department of Architecture where we have endeavoured over the past fifteen years to provide a critique of the contemporary built environment.[1] (Fig 1) One of the recurring themes of the studio has been the history of work places and the spatial consequences of de-industrialisation, issues that informed G.L.A.S' contribution to the international travelling exhibition Shrinking Cities and the development of the S.O.L project[2]. (Fig 2)

S.O.L began life as a series of mapping exercises. Students were asked to select a natural resource or commodity, research it and then develop a strategy for the transformation of the built environment based around the history and production of their chosen subject.

JONATHAN CHARLEY

The projects displayed in the exhibition and explored in more detail in the catalogue and website represent only a sample of the work produced, but are nevertheless representative of the different types of response that vary from the development of new forms of agricultural production to ideas for new building typologies. For example the investigations into coal and fishing are primarily observational and document the traces of vanishing lives, the work on seaweed, slate and recycling are propositional, whereas the projects that feature broad rural and urban panoramas are clearly speculative and try to envision more general transformations in our agricultural and industrial landscapes.

The Architecture of Work

Of all the profound changes and upheavals that hit northern Europe in the latter quarter of the twentieth century and which signalled the end of the post world war two expansionary wave of capital accumulation, it is probably the process of de-industrialisation that had the greatest impact on the social and economic welfare of communities. The crisis that enveloped the UK economy in the nineteen seventies and eighties caused irreparable damage to the social fabric of Britain. It tore families apart and destroyed individual lives. The ensuing social and economic catastrophe prompted economists and sociologists to re-examine the social and technological history of the capitalist labour process and to re-engage with debates about the dynamics of capital accumulation.[3] But whilst the social history and critique of work gathered pace, there seemed to be something missing. That absence was the notion of geography, of space, and of architecture, the reality that capital accumulation and production possess both temporal and spatial dimensions. (Fig 3)

This was particularly important for understanding the devastating flight of capital and the spatial restructuring of the division of labour that occurred from the 1970s onwards and finally put paid to the remnants of heavy and light industry in Scotland including the slate, fishing, coal and textiles industries. However although considerable energy went into understanding the geographical dimensions of capitalist production in terms of the socio-spatial division of particular branches of industrial production and manufacturing, very little attention was devoted to the design of actual work buildings, which to date still represents the biggest omission in most histories of architecture and building.

This is all the more remarkable when we think that for those of us in regular employment we spend a third of our adult lives at work. Until the shift in the nineteen seventies when historians began to reflect upon the architecture of everyday life, most architectural history had been confined to distinctions and judgments of taste or monographs about particular

Fig 1 — G.L.A.S and its agit-prop truck
at the Govanhill Pool Occupation, 2001

Fig 2 —'Industrial' palette of G.L.A.S
Paper 08 on Industrialisation, Shrinking Cities
Exhibition Berlin 2003

architects and their iconic buildings. Typical books on the history of architecture in Scotland might well contain an image of Templeton's 'Venetian' Carpet factory or Gardner's pioneering cast-iron warehouse in Glasgow but it is unlikely that they would devote more than a few pages out of hundreds to industrial architecture and work buildings.[4] Such books tell us virtually nothing about the illustrious MacFarlane's Foundry and Saracen works that pre-cast iron buildings for export all over the world and supported a population of fifty thousand people in the north of Glasgow, or the equally grand Singer machine factory in Clydebank that manufactured sewing machines for the world market. (Fig 4) Not surprisingly even fewer examples exist of historians who have sought to penetrate beyond the facades of such 'industrial' buildings to understand how capitalist work practices were organised spatially on the shop floor in both a social and technological sense. This is work that still needs to be done.[5] The work of S.O.L represents one very small contribution to this project.

Memory and Heritage

How we remember, commemorate, and record our social and architectural history is one of the central concerns of the S.O.L project. As in all history the question arises as to whose history is being recalled and how it is being represented. Although in the field of social history considerable progress was made during the latter half of the twentieth century in ensuring that working class history, women's history and the history of the marginalised and excluded found its way onto the library shelves, the physical and material history of working class culture in Britain has been less satisfactorily dealt with.

Although there is now a European wide organisation that is seeking to document and in some cases preserve the remnants of nineteenth century and twentieth century industrial production there is a feeling that we are somehow embarrassed about this aspect of our history in Britain.[6] Compare for instance what we have done or rather ignored and demolished in the central belt of Scotland and what has been

accomplished in the Ruhr valley in Germany. (Fig 5) There they have created a seven hundred kilometre network of canals, footpaths and cycle ways that link the former sites of coal, chemical, steel and iron production into an extraordinary industrial park joining Duisburg in the west with Dortmund in the East.[7] This is the equivalent of joining up the mills of Paisley with the coalfields of Fife and Lothian to create a green corridor that celebrates industrial culture and that stretches across the whole of the central belt of Scotland.

If this sounds implausible imagine one of the largest cast iron and steel works in the Ruhr reopened as a public park with climbing walls, a pool, and bars. Imagine club nights taking place inside gasometers, diving centres in water storage towers, pithead baths transformed into restaurants, bings turned into viewing platforms, and steel washing basins into winter ice rinks. Not only that imagine forty metre high towers, furnaces and engineering structures that the public is free to roam over and ascend to gaze across the whole of the Ruhr valley.[8] In contrast there isn't a trace of the cathedral size structures that once dominated the horizon around Ravenscraig, or the extraordinary brick buildings such as the Granaries and the Harland and Wolff yards that once flanked the Clyde.

It is as if in the vain battle to re-image Glasgow as a vibrant post-industrial city, all remnants of its working class and rebellious history have to be physically removed from the urban landscape apart from the odd sad and solitary crane. (Fig 6) The reason often given for the demolition of such monuments to industrial prowess is that there was no obvious way of re-using these structures. However this was often little more than a mask for a paucity of imagination and the fact that they stood on potentially valuable real estate.

There is of course a danger when dealing with industrial history of fetishising it and turning everything into a theme park where the visitor gets a taste of coal and steel in the midst of a gift and souvenir shop (although even this is better than there being no trace what so ever).

Fig 3 — Gable end wall celebrating the Saracen Works, North Glasgow.

Fig 4 — Cast Iron water fountain, one of a number of structures exported all over the world from Glasgow.

It is equally important to be wary of romanticising working life in the pits, steel industry and shipyards. It took generations of organised struggle to improve working conditions and even then work was hard. Neither would we want to objectify the landscapes that emerged from these often toxic processes of industrial production as art objects. However it is hard to deny the extraordinary phenomenological quality and impact of these sites of industrial construction that even if they weren't built with an artists' intent nevertheless were testaments to extraordinary engineering skill and craftsmanship. (Fig 7)

Either way the majority of our industrial heritage has been swept away making it all the more important that we try and deal creatively with what's left of Scotland's industrial past including preserving the oral memories of those who are still alive and remember what it was like to work in the factories, mills and yards.[9] It is after all human labour in all its creative guises making tangible commodities that ultimately produces wealth, not as we have seen the extraordinary baroque mechanisms of the finance markets.

The Crisis Of Neo-Liberalism

Alongside questions of historical memory and the architecture of work, the critique of the neo-liberal project lies at the heart of the S.O.L agenda. Neo-liberal economic policy was driven by three deeply ideological obsessions; trade liberalisation, the pursuit of (largely mythological) free markets, and privatisation. This as we know greatly accelerated the process of local industrial decline, the consequences of which in Scotland were devastating in terms of the corrosive effects of long-term unemployment and poverty.

However the story of closures, redundancies and 'geographical switch' in the pursuit of cheaper labour power is as old as capitalism itself. Indeed it is one of ways in which capitalism periodically restructures itself when faced with a decline in profitability and the threat of economic crisis. It is a tragic tale that has been replayed throughout the twentieth century

in Scotland, a century that began with the decline of the textile industry put out of business by the importation of cheaper fabrics and ended with the virtual eradication of heavy industry that was unable to compete in the global market for steel, ships, or cars. (Fig 8)

And if more evidence were needed of the fickle nature of capital investment we only have to remember the echoes of the much vaunted 'silicon glen' that was going to revitalise Scotland's economy through electronics along with the equally exaggerated claims of the 'call centre' revolution that quickly ran into trouble as firms relocated to India.[10] This economic opportunism is the leitmotif of capitalist development. It comes as little surprise then that capital in the twenty first century is no more loyal to employees and regions trying to rebuild an economy through new information and financial services than it was during earlier periods of industrial expansion. It is simply that capital being mobile and amoral will inevitably seek out regions where it can rent land and produce such commodities more cheaply. This all suggests that the idea that Scotland like the regions of England can regenerate its economy through a combination of civic boosterism, tourism, retail and service industries is at best wishful thinking and at worst myopic.

Although economic planning and forms of public ownership are not panaceas or guarantees of economic survival in a global and competitive world economic system, it is equally the case that leaving it to largely unregulated markets does not provide a solution. In fact despite what we hear, far from being 'free' these markets are in reality regulated just as the economic activities of major corporations are planned, it is simply that they are regulated and planned in line with the profit interests of directors and shareholders rather than in the social interests of the broad mass of the population.

There are alternatives even within the context of capitalist economic development to a service based economy. There is still a need for coal and steel. But even if it is unlikely that we will be either able or willing to reopen pits and steel mills, there is clearly an alternative to old school

Fig 5 – Beer and five asides in the ruins of a former steel plant, Ruhr valley, Germany.

Fig 6 – Derelict football pitch, Yarrow yard, Glasgow.

heavy industrial production that is informed not least by the imperatives placed upon us by climate change and threats to our immediate social and environmental survival. There is no shortage of imagination and creativity within the economy, what we need is political will and economic investment.

The S.O.L project then is self consciously idealistic and considers it imperative that we begin to think more creatively not just about what we do with the remains of past enterprises but about new possibilities for transforming our built environment whether urban or rural, hence the subtitle for this exhibition "re-imagining a productive landscape for Scotland". It might not be immediately commercially viable to reopen slate quarries, generate power from harbour walls, farm dyes from indigenous crops, or build recycling centres to manufacture green building materials, but there is no reason why we shouldn't begin to speculate about what new types of industrial and agricultural production could develop that exploit Scotland's abundant resources.

The point being that the global division of labour upon which capitalism operates can change radically and swiftly. When the central belt of Scotland was renowned as one of the industrial powerhouses of the world economy, there were few who could have thought or imagined that in the space of two generations it would be reduced to a virtually invisible ruin. It is not difficult to imagine a scenario spinning out over the next couple of decades where Chinese and Indian labour costs rise, the Korean ship building industry ceases to be competitive, energy and transportation costs rise exponentially, new environmental imperatives emerge, hitherto unseen conflicts erupt and any number of bank crises, stock market crashes occur that will throw the world economy into a bout of seizures with unknown consequences. Such a sequence of events will demand a very different response from national governments. But changes in economic and environmental priorities need not be provoked by catastrophe. They can be planned, democratically and with care and foresight as to potential long term advantages rather than what guides current economic policy which is pragmatic political expediency and

short term profits. A simple shift in government policy can radically alter both industrial and environmental landscapes.[11] Crucially architecture has an important role to play here in terms of documentation, strategic planning and providing a visual language to accompany the possibility of new places of work and industrial production. Ultimately, despite the bizarre claims made about the nature of 'knowledge' led economies, and miraculous 'cure all' service sectors, it is impossible to imagine a productive society and a healthy economy without a vibrant manufacturing sector making useful things.[12]

Landscapes of Production

It is apposite given the twenty-fifth anniversary of the miner's strike that part of the exhibition is devoted to the history of the coal industry. Although we now have a Scottish mining museum near Newtongrange, it is difficult within a single museum to capture the profound influence of coal production on the Scottish landscape. For many perhaps it is a history that they would rather forget. But for others it represents a proud chapter in working class history. Either way as the photographic study shows we have virtually eradicated all traces of how the coal industry impacted and formed part of the Scottish landscape. A few of the winding gears remain, the odd bing, but virtually all of the modernist pithead baths which nowadays would probably be listed and protected as buildings of architectural merit have long since been demolished. The project on the history of fishing also takes the form of a photographic survey of nearly two hundred harbours down the east coast of Scotland. Virtually all of them are now disused, put out of business by the capitalisation and industrialisation of the fishing industry and the development of massive factory ships. Despite this, such a photographic record raises a number of important rhetorical questions about what we find of historical value and how in this particular instance hundreds of years of industry and the memories of thousands of families is in danger of being erased. It also poses questions about the future and the opportunities that we are missing to develop an alternative maritime culture along the six thousand miles of Scottish coastline. [13] The work on

Fig 7 – Crane in the remains of the John Brown Yard, Clydebank.

Fig 8 – Ruins of Vale of Leven mill.

11

Seaweed provides a partial response to this dilemma and suggests that with appropriate investment and political will there is no reason why a thriving seaweed industry could not develop off the marine areas on the west coast providing much needed employment that is environmentally sensitive, self sustaining in terms of energy requirements and designed in a manner that points to the possibility of a contemporary maritime vernacular architecture.

In a similar spirit the projects on slate and paper recycling ask questions about the relationship between old and new industries. Slate is one of the most long lasting and durable construction materials we have. Although there is a finite supply within the earth there is enough to roof Scotland for centuries. It is also reusable and recyclable. The main reason that the slate industry closed in Scotland was because of the availability of cheaper slate and composite products from abroad along with the development of the concrete roof tile, both of which were cheaper to produce and highly profitable for the manufacturing firms involved. Although such substitutes are reasonably long lasting, they are incomparable in terms of longevity and the extraordinary blue, grey, purple aesthetic qualities of indigenous Scottish slate. In addition although the slate industry wasn't the biggest employer in the building industry, areas that historically developed in close connection with the industry such as at Ballachulish experienced a relative economic catastrophe with the closure of the quarries. It is clearly possible with advanced cutting and mining technology to rework them, just as quarries were reopened to provide indigenous stone for the construction of the Scottish parliament

As for timber and paper, we hear much about recycling but very little about any creative engagement with how it could become an important part of economic regeneration. As hopefully the papercrete project demonstrates not only is it possible to recycle waste paper to produce a variety of commodities with potential applications within the building industry but with very distinctive and innovative aesthetic qualities that are dependent on the quality, colour and texture of the paper used.

The two other projects on show take a slightly different approach. The first collages a sequence of utopian scenarios that re-imagines Glasgow in the future, re-invented as a twenty first century eco-industrial city. The second is more of a methodological statement that can be applied to other regions. It starts by mapping a slice of Scotland from Ardnamurchan to Fife, locates natural resources, speculates about what types of commodities could be produced and then imagines in a sequence of four panoramic images what new types of rural and maritime landscape could emerge.

Clearly the sectors of the economy that S.O.L has begun to investigate represent a small fragment of the Scottish economy and landscape, but we hope that the exhibition and catalogue make a constructive contribution to the debate about Scotland's economic and social future and the role that architecture can play.

Jonathan Charley

1 — Over the twenty years I have been teaching architecture I have endeavoured to synthesise a politically radical and socially engaged programme with a commitment to formal and technological innovation. Critical engagement for me is the whole point of education. It should aspire to asking impossible 'what if' questions, to speculating about uncertain and unpredictable futures. It should resemble a voyage into the unknown organised in the spirit of an experimental laboratory. Like S.O.L, G,L.A.S was organised and registered as a co-operative. We ran a paper for five years, organised workshops and participated in a number of actions and exhibitions. G.L.A.S' first project the Urban Cabaret, involved the transformation of Piaggio Ape van into an agit-prop vehicle that we drove around Glasgow distributing copies of the paper, making tea and engaging with community struggles such as the campaign to save the Govanhill Pool. See website for more information and an archive of G.L.A.S activities. www.glaspaper.com

2 — See Glaspaper 08, GLASPAPER 08, Spaces of Labour-Arbeitsstatten, Summer, 2004, ISSN 1476-3206. www.glaspaper.com

3 — For a classic and more recent summary and critique of post Second World War economic history see Mandel, Ernest, Late Capitalism, Verso, London, 1999 (1972) and Brenner, Robert, The Economics of global turbulence- A special report of the world economy, 1950-1998, NLR, No 229, 1998. It was in the 1970s that attention was refocused on the technological and social history of the capitalist labour process. Amongst other things it looked at the impact of new technology on productivity and the necessary re-skilling of workforces, at the extent of political control of the means of production, and at the introduction of new forms of work place organisation and management. See the collected Proceedings of the B.I.S.S, Bartlett International Summer School, Volumes 1-17, 1979-1995, ISBN 0 903 109 various, that contain numerous articles on the labour process in general but in particular its historical transformation in the construction industry. Three useful introductions at the time were Littler, Craig, The development of the Labour Process in capitalist societies, Gower, Aldershot -1982, Mackenzie and Wajcman, J, The social shaping of technology, OUP, 1988, and Burawoy, Michael, The Politics of production - Factory regimes under capitalism and socialism, Verso, 1985

4 — To take two well known books on the architectural history of Scotland. See for instance A history of Scottish Architecture, Glendinning, MacInnes and MacKechnie, Edinburgh University Press, 1997, or The Buildings of Scotland; Glasgow, Williamson, Riches and Higgs, Penguin 1990.

5 — One of the exceptions is Tom Markus' analysis of industrial buildings in Buildings and Power; The origins of Freedom and Control in Modern Building Types (1993) There is in contrast a growing body of works that looks at the health risks and problems associated with particular working environments. Asbestosis lying at one end of the spectrum and new types of 'sick building syndrome associated with sealed office environments at the other. See for instance numerous articles by Taylor, P and Bain P including Trade Unions and sick building syndrome- The developing struggle for workers health, in Resistance, Proceedings of the B.I.S.S, Bartlett International Summer School, Volumes 17, 1979-1995, ISBN 0 903 109 38 7

6 — See ERIH, European Route of Industrial Heritage www.erih.net

7 — See the website http://www.route-industriekultur.de for a detailed map and guide. Two highlights are the Zollverein coal plant now a UNESCO world heritage site, and the giant former iron and steel works at the Landschaftspark Duisburg-Nord.

8 — Remarkably the pig iron pits near Bochum now have a preservation order since they boast a floral subculture featuring species of flowers and plants that are only found in South Africa where much of the original iron ore was mined.

9 — See for instance the work of McIvor, Arthur et al Scottish Oral History Project, University of Strathclyde.

10 — In fact call centre companies have even less commitment to local economies than old 'industrial' capitalists. Indeed the absence of any need to invest extensively in fixed capital makes it easier for them to relocate. However in the past even this didn't stop legendary capitalist adventurers like the Angus Jute Works in Dundee that in 1919, dismantled their looms shipped them across the world and re-erected them in factories on the Hoogly Delta in Kolkata.

11 — Following the Brasilian governments initiatives over recent years a remarkable seventy five per cent of all fuel sold for domestic cars in is already being produced from bio crops like sugar cane which will mean in the very near future Brasil will be free from oil dependence in the light vehicle sector.

12 — Although manufacturing still figures more highly in the Scottish economy than some might think, it still only accounts for a about a quarter of economic activity.

13 — A useful contribution to the debate about Scotland's untapped coastline was made in the exhibition and catalogue 6000 Miles hosted by the Lighthouse Scotland's Centre for Architecture and Design. See Six Thousand Miles, Exhibition Catalogue, The Lighthouse, Glasgow, April 2005, ISBN 1-905061-05-6

14 — To take one more profoundly contradictory example of the way in which contemporary capitalism operates; in the on going mission to repave the city centre of Glasgow it has proved cheaper to mine the granite in China and ship it across the world than to employ local craftsmen by reopening quarries in Scotland.

THE PITS

My village was surrounded by walking and cycling paths, which helpfully connected us to nearby villages in straight and level routes. When we were wee we used to go walking and cycling looking for whatever we could get: brambles; raspberries; hazelnuts; peas; tatties; itchy powder (rosehip), pee the beds (dandelions), conkers and tadpoles. Along the route were occasional grey stones etched with details of no importance. There were two great bridges built of brick arches carrying roads above them, it didn't occur to us the great effort that had been made to by-pass our path. At Guides we had sausage sizzles on a raised brick platform that looked over the path, while overlooking us were black and white metal ladders with protective loops around them. Further along the path were the bings, big black mounds which were high, steep and hard to climb up but always busy with scramble bikes.

Fifteen years later I realised that my rural idyll was manufactured.

LAURA HAINEY

I grew up in a former coalmining village in Scotland and both sides of my family have a background in the mining industry. While growing up I had heard many tales, often jokes from my dad and uncles about working in "the pits" and had formed in my head an imagined landscape of shafts and cages, conveyors and baths. I visited the Ruhr valley in Germany and walking round Zeche Zollern Colliery in Dortmund and Zollverein Colliery in Essen I was finally able to provide a tangible base for the stories I had heard as a child.

On return from Germany I began to wonder what had happened to the collieries that dotted the central belt of Scotland and employed a large proportion of the population. Why did we only have one Mining Museum and two smaller heritage sites when the Ruhr Valley has six such sites that form part of a heritage network of former industrial sites and buildings that are fully accessible by the public? What did remain from the mining Industry in Scotland and did we have a rich Architectural heritage to show for it? Why was it not celebrated in the same proud way?

This project sought to uncover by means of black and white photography what was left of the built environment associated with the Scottish mining Industry so as to gain a view of this part of the Post-Productive Landscape in Scotland.

Scotland was home to numerous notable colliery buildings. In the Victorian era competing coal companies vied for top production figures by employing the most up to date machinery and methods, often imported from the continent.

This led to several "showpiece" collieries such as Comrie Colliery in Fife where an ornamental pond doubled as the cooling system for brakes and Lady Victoria Colliery in Newtongrange whose ornate brickwork survives today.

In the 1920s the Miners Welfare Fund brought about two distinctive building typologies: Miners Welfare's - social clubs and libraries built to a domestic scale and situated within existing town and villages; and Pithead Baths, modern structures of brick, concrete and glass, constructed as monuments to cleanliness and efficiency that were built on the colliery sites.

In the post war years the coal industry in the UK was both nationalised and rationalised. Only profitable pits were brought in to the National Coal Board Scheme and a grand scheme of new sinkings planned. The "Superpits" designed by the NCB Architect Egon Riss dotted the central belt, proud concrete and glass buildings, where health and safety were of paramount concern.

Gargantuan towers of concrete and glass often dominated the skyline, visible for miles looking down on cubic fanhouses with iconic curved chimneys, aerial walkways, austere inward looking pithead baths and intimidating office complexes.

Coal is a finite resource

The Nationalisation of the Coal Industry brought about better provision for the workers and several optimistic "Superpit" schemes; that employed thousands of workers., However, the NCI also funded the construction of ambitious iconic and permanent buildings for what were often temporary endeavours, and encouraged the continued existence, through political legislation, of single industry towns.

The demise of the coal industry during the 1980s led to the demolition of the collieries, the sale of machinery the selling or letting of the land for other ventures and widespread unemployment. Very rarely did the new owners see a viable use for the existing buildings. The bitter sentiment harboured by almost wholly unemployed towns nearby did nothing to ensure the survival of the colliery buildings. This coupled with the unfortunate reality that industrial architecture is often not appreciated led to the almost full scale destruction of the pit buildings in Scotland.

Against the odds a few of the former pit buildings have survived in the central belt of Scotland. Some have been given a new lease of life as museums and heritage sites, others as industrial sites and businesses, and one has even been transformed into a home. In other instances only a part of the colliery survives often hidden and in rare cases preserved as a stand alone monument in a park. Some of the examples shown on the next few pages however are at risk or earmarked for demolition.

Between September 2008 and March 2009 I visited 22 former collieries in Ayrshire, Fife, Clackmannanshire and the Lothians with my father, many of them were his, my uncles' or my grandfathers' former workplaces.

I also visited one example of an early drift mine in an Industrial Heritage site in Lanarkshire. With the aid of my Dad's memory, the directions of old men smoking outside Miner's Welfares and some road maps from the 1980s we were able to locate the majority of the pits I sought to find.

I documented each site using black and white 35mm film photography in order to provide a direct comparison with the archive images that exist of the collieries in a working state. Black and White photography was also used as it allows the eye to directly appreciate form and texture and not be distracted by colour of foliage or evidence of building decay. Each image for the final collection was printed by hand in the dark room.

Left – Monktonhall Colliery Midlothian.
Right – Prestongrange Museum, Prestonpans, East Lothian.

Left – Bing near East Lothian.
Right – Tynemount Bing, Ormiston, East Lothian.

Clockwise from top left – Headgear with coal fired power station in the background, Prestongrange. The only surviving Concrete headgear, The Mary Colliery, now Lochore Meadows country park. Highhouse Colliery, Auchinleck.

Opposite – Wooden headgear, Summerlee Heritage Park, Coatbridge.

Left – Fanhouse, Rothes Colliery, near Thornton, Glenrothes, Fife.
Right – Pithead baths, Prestongrange Museum, East Lothian.

Clockwise from top left – The offices, The Killoch, near Ochiltree. Headgear, The Barony, near Auchinleck. Enterkine No. 9 & 10 former Pithead Baths, now a house, near Annbank.

Views of Coal preparation Plant, derelict and earmarked for demolition, near New Cumnock.

Views of Castlehill Colliery, Fife, The Ramsay,
Loanhead Midlothian and Comrie Colliery, Fife.

Clockwise from top left – Lady Victoria Colliery, Scottish Mining Museum, Newtongrange. Stone commemorating Bellyford Pit. Railway Walk (Howden), Ormiston. "In Gaun E'e" entrance to a drift mine, Summerlee Heritage Park, Coatbridge.

Opposite – Road and railway hoppers, coal prep plant, wnear New Cumnock.

INDUSTRIAL MONUMENTS

This idea for this journey stemmed from a Diploma exploration into the re-invigoration of a small fishing town. I wanted to expand the geographical, social and historical context in which my earlier work had been set. This led me to plan a journey along the entire East coast of Scotland, recording as many harbours, piers and jetties as was possible. The following pages include only a selection of the 200 harbours and slips I documented, the rest are viewable on the Spaces of Labour website. What is interesting about visiting such a large number of harbours is the variety. Harbour forms are always different and dependent on the sea and surrounding landscape. The East coast harbours are exciting, unique structures in themselves. Skeletal functional objects that represent man's eternal battle with the sea. The harbours are monumental, historical and marvels of engineering. At their most basic level they can be considered to be landscape architecture merging with the sea.

THOMAS BOOTH

One of the key moments in the development of the East Coast harbours was in 1700 when the British Fishing Association was set up, allowing money to be made available for the construction of boats, piers and harbour walls. As the industry grew, more boats were needed and of a larger size. Harbours grew, with major extensions to existing walls. Buildings were constructed to deal with the handling, storing, smoking, curing and packing of fish for export. Scotland now had the largest fishing industry in Europe and was exporting barrelled herring even as far as Russia. For the fishermen and fishwives it was a hard life, working long days in all weather conditions.

The fishing life was nomadic, dependent on the season and availability of work. Fishing folk would travel up and down the East coast, as far South as Yarmouth, across the country to Mallaig and beyond to Ireland. Over the years, boat and net technology advanced, allowing fishing to take place farther out at sea and greater hauls to be reeled in. This meant harbours expanded to accommodate ever larger fleets of fishing vessels.

There were many reasons for the decline of the traditional fishing industry organised around family and kinships groups. One of them was the development of new steam boats that operated with less men and could pull in far greater hauls. Fish processing could be done inside the safety of the vessel rather than on the deck and this was eventually to lead to the development of the factory trawlers and super-trawlers we see today.

Nowadays, many old harbours on the East coast are still operational in one form or another. They have in many places changed their use from fishing ports to places where people keep pleasure boats such as yachts and dinghies. Old harbours such as Aberdeen and Leith, now deal mainly with the oil industry and commercial trade. It is interesting to note that whereas prosperity was once measured by fishing stocks, advances in boat technology and infrastructure have led to prosperity being marked by geographical location.

In order to create a photographic analysis, several journeys to the East coast were necessary. This involved research using the Ordnance Survey and Bartholomew's maps of Scotland. There were many places where little or nothing now remains; these were once small fishing communities, historical landing points, or piers. Some places indicated only a past fishing history, often based on the layout of a narrow street with houses on either side, leading down to the shore. Some places were inaccessible due to cliffs and difficult access along the coastline. Some locations have not been recorded due to security restrictions, such as at Grangemouth and Dounray, or for other commercial, industrial or military reasons.

The original idea was to assess the difference in the harbours along the coast. Each area of coastline had its own characteristics, and even over a small stretch this could change quite dramatically. In the past the harbours were used for the import and export of goods, as well as the catching and landing of fish, but many harbours have now been adapted to accommodate newer industries such as oil, nuclear power, container transport, pleasure boats and naval use. At some places you can still find small creel boats, that are used for the part time fishing of crab or lobsters, one of the few reminders of what was once a locally run vibrant fishing industry. In addition in most small harbours or slips, and even on some beaches and natural inlets, you will still find the odd two-man boat. But average sized trawlers are in danger of becoming extinct since they simply can't compete with the super-trawlers.

What is evident from this journey is that, while the larger boats may be efficient and economically viable, they come at the expense not only of destroying the economic livelihood of small villages but of over-fishing the sea. Even though older methods and smaller boats may be more environmentally viable, there is an argument that many more people would be working in the industry and that some smaller harbours could be revived as fishing centres. In reality this will probably only happen if stocks become too low to bulk fish and if a cap is put on the number and size of intensive sea-farming vessels. What is interesting to note is that relatively few fishermen blame fishing itself for the lack of fish. Excuses range from "it's the dolphins that eat them all these days" or "it's the Spanish!"; also at fault are "the Portuguese", and one blamed Ted Heath for bringing us into the EU. Only a few are prepared to admit that the North sea has been overfished, and that it was "New methods of fishing and the greed of man" (Gwyn Tanner, Avoch harbour master) that has partly caused the decline.

In fact, many of the harbours could be redefined and reused. There is an argument to retain what is there, without giving it a temporary makeover. With the reintroduction and promotion of new, greener and small scale coastal industries, these harbours and their communities will thrive once again. This approach stems from historical precedent and is important to maintain the coastline's identity.

The research journey was made in several stages over a period of months. Some places had to be revisited if photographs were poor due to bad light or unsuitable weather conditions. Local knowledge proved extremely valuable and allowed newer and now forgotten places to be captured. Finding the harbours sometimes involved trips down rough farm tracks and a walk over fields, looking over cliff edges and knocking on the doors of remote houses to ask for directions.

Without the locational recording of Scotland's epic story with the sea, this history will die. Heritage is not just found in a museum. It is the harbours, villages and landscapes which belong to a past industry that has declined. To acknowledge the importance of these places would be a worthy celebration of the culture surrounding Scotland's fishing community.

Pittenweem

Scrabster

Peterhead

Blackness Castle

Methil

Aberdeen

Hawes Pier

Belhaven

Fraserburgh

Alloa

Seacliff

Latheronwheel

Skirza

Arbroath

Anstruther

Crail

Collieston

Portsoy

Gills Bay

Embo

Limekilns

Whaligoe

Sarclet

Auckengill

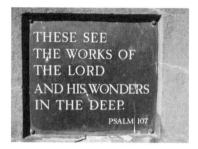

47

RE-IMAGINING A PRODUCTIVE LANDSCAPE

LIAM MADDEN & IAIN THOMSON

The project 're-imagining a productive landscape' had its origins in our diploma work where we investigated the history and fate of the textile industry in the Cumbernauld area. This resulted in series of proposals to build a twenty first century textile mill coupled with a research centre for the production of dyes. It was our intention that these buildings would run using alternative energy and would produce commodities made out of materials and resources indigenous to the Scottish landscape. This led us to speculate on how it might be possible to extend such a logic to the whole of the Scottish economy; a highly idealised scenario in which a new manufacturing and energy-producing sector emerges that produces things for domestic and world markets using only Scottish resources. As a pilot exercise we took a strip across Scotland from the Ardnamurchan peninsular to Fife and began to map what natural resources are available and what they could potentially be transformed into, whether it be new foods, construction materials, textiles, or pharmaceuticals. To try and capture the implications of such a plan for the built environment we produced a series of maps showing new networks and infrastructure and four 'what if' imaginary views of a Scottish landscape devoted to the production of energy and the manufacturing of goods.

Oceanic, Moorland

Montane, Freshwater

Tundra, Montane, Moorland

Moorland, Estuarine, Oceanic

FROM THE GALLERY WALL
TO THE VILLAGE HALL

In response to the general decline of industry within Scotland, the premise of the Spaces of Labour unit was to envisage a new productive landscape based on a native resource. I chose seaweed on a hunch that it was an under-used but valuable resource which has the potential to form the basis of a unique architectural project.

Seaweed has a wide variety of uses from fuel production and fertilisers to cosmetics and foodstuffs. There has also been extensive research into new and future uses for seaweed as a source of biofuel, an additive to fatty foods to combat obesity and even as a building material. Scotland hosts around 20% of the total seaweed biomass in Europe, yet only harvests 2% of this share. Around 50% of Scotland's seaweed stocks can be found in the North West Highlands, so the most obvious location for a new seaweed industry would be within this area.

JAMES TAIT

The coastal village of Arisaig will be the location for this new development for three main reasons; The area has a long history of seaweed use both domestic and industrial dating back over 300 years; Its location and sheltered bay provides the ideal environment for the cultivation of seaweed and its beauty and tranquillity offer the perfect surroundings for a sensitive and proportionate project looking to incorporate leisure, industry and health.

The final proposal comprises of : An offshore seaweed farm; seeding lab; steam drying tower; seaweed steam baths; packaging warehouse; individual seaweed farmer stations; a boat yard; workers' social space; a new pier; and a restaurant. These structures explore all aspects of the proposed industry through cultivation, production and consumption while establishing a varied and sensitive industry based on an abundant and natural resource.

My 'Time and Tide for Seaweed' project managed to win a number of national and international awards. Despite this rise in stock within the architectural world, I heard some sage advice from my tutors ringing in my ears: " you need to go up and see what the locals make of it." Tentatively, I begun to map out the steps required to take my project into the communities and landscapes it was intended for.

The first step was to post flyers through the doors of the 70 or so homes in Arisaig to publicise an exhibition of my work in the local visitors centre. Posters were placed in community signboards and an article on my project was published in the local paper the 'West Word'.

Finally, there was a meeting with the twelve or so members of the Arisaig Community Trust at the local Village hall, a recently formed local community focus group...

RC - What's going to happen to the yachts in the bay? No-one's going to come to Arisaig to see a seaweed factory!

JT - If I was proposing a seaweed 'factory' I would completely agree with you. I have added in other elements incorporating health, leisure and tourism such as the restaurant and seaweed baths. I believe people would come to see them.

JW - The whole project doesn't look very nice. It's impact is horrible. The buildings are not really rural. You need to put more sympathy into the design. You can still do that because you've got computers and you can change it, can't you? You need to go back down.

JT - What do you think would improve it?

JW - Well stay here in Arisaig and absorb it and you'll think woah I could do it completely different now. Or not do it at all!

JT - I have looked at traditional materials and traditional coastal forms. The drying tower was based on lighthouse forms and the seaweed baths are clad in the exact same material (black-stained timber) as the building we are standing in at the moment.

MW - Why not somewhere else like Loch Nan Uamh...no-one lives there. You've put it in a place where a lot of people live and it would spoil the view completely.

LB - There are a lot of other villages looking to fund projects, you know.

Following this rather deflating but worthwhile meeting, I then spoke with the Highland Planning Department and the Scottish Association of Marine Scientists in order to discuss the viability of my proposals. Again a healthy dose of reality was administered by both.

The planning department raised numerous issues, both specific and general. The existing chunky stone pier was to be retained as a means of flood defence, rendering the new pier and restaurant redundant, the height of the lighthouse-esque drying tower would not be permitted as a rule within the guidelines which states that no new development is allowed to break the line between land and sky, and finally that the form and materials used were not 'rural' enough. When pressed on this issue the planner in question stated that "bog standard white render and a pitched slate roof" would be preferred.

The marine scientists stated that the cultivation raft poles were unnecessary as the Crown Estates will charge for each pole embedded in the seabed. Standard buoys were advised instead. This would effectively eliminate one of the most important aspects of the original design, the glowing poles of light across the bay. A combination of Salmon and Seaweed farming was also advised to ensure profitability, that would

change the productive landscape of the scheme dramatically. I was also informed that the 'corten' steel cladding used would contaminate the seaweed. Ironically, the component of the consultation which seemed to have the least impact on aesthetics in fact had the most.

My findings were fed into the original design and allow me to imagine three separate scenarios relating to my project. The utopian, the dystopian and the dialectical alternative. These will serve to illustrate the contrast between the lofty ideals of the designer with the wariness and fear of the rural community of Arisaig and how this resistance to change could affect the village and other communities like it forever.

An alternative scenario is also proposed that uses the opinions of planning and marine scientists as a tool to visualise the impact economics, public opinion, land use and technicalities could have on the original design.

I now understand what could be improved on my original design, but also that many of the issues raised were either out-with my control or out-with my sphere of knowledge. This is evident in many of my discoveries, be it the lack of enthusiasm from the community, the tendency for the Highland planning department to discourage designs which don't adhere to a perceived notion of history, or the fact that one of the key features of my design (the cultivation rafts and poles) would have to be significantly altered due to regulations imposed by the Crown Estate.

Ultimately these discoveries would not have been identified without my carrying out the process of taking my project into reality.

Another facet of this study is the attitude of certain groups within Highland communities, who can often appear to be resistant to change and development. This was evident in the meeting with the Arisaig Community Trust who clearly fear that any development industrial or otherwise would besmirch their rural idyll.

I believe that rural development should not be feared. It should be welcomed, and if it comes in the form of a natural, diverse and profitable industry such as a seaweed industry, then all the better. However, in order for rural Highland development to occur, architects and students of architecture must embrace factors out-with their control and trained sensibilities resisting a tendency towards utopianism, our planning system has to become more open to designs which do not subscribe to a false notion of history , and most importantly these rural communities must recognise if they do not adapt, possible extinction awaits.

To do anything less would be a disservice to a once thriving and peopled landscape which has become a man made wilderness formed by centuries of conflict, clearance, restrictive planning and a consistently hierarchical society.

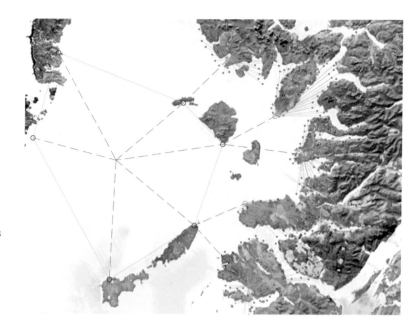

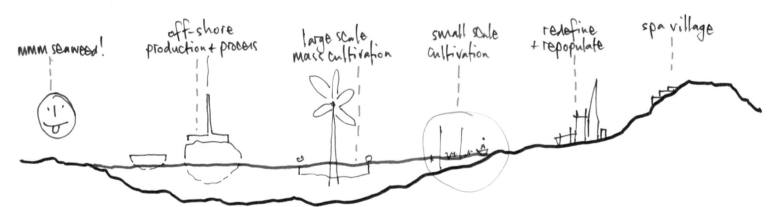

mmm seaweed!

off-shore production + process

large scale mass cultivation

small scale cultivation

redefine + repopulate

spa village

Top – ALGAE-NET: Diagram of a seaweed industry as the generator for a trade and transportation network connecting remote areas within the North West Highlands.

Above – A preparatory study investigating seaweed as a natural resource, process and product and the physical manifestations of each.

Opposite – Aerial perspective of the cultivation farm and its offshoots, demonstrating how the project responds to its natural environment.

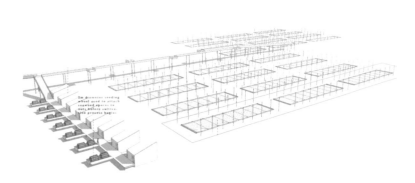

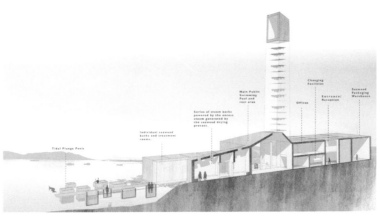

Cultivation – Detailed analysis of seaweed farm incorporating boat stations and seaweed cultivation rafts.

Production – Detailed analysis of public seaweed baths and drying tower complex using steam to provide the energy needed for both functions.

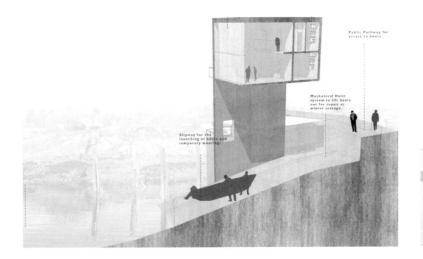

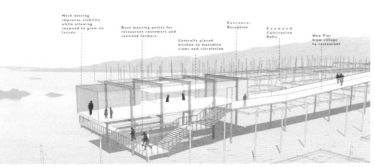

Provision – Detailed analysis of Farmers Bothy highlighting materiality, tectonics and social relations.

Consumption – Detailed analysis of floating seaweed restaurant and its relationship to its surrounding landscape and parasitical nature of the base resource.

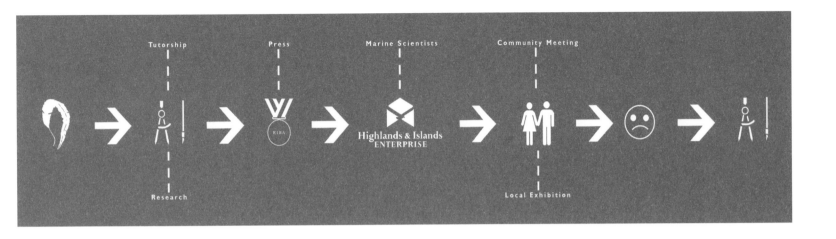

Tutorship

Press

Marine Scientists

Community Meeting

RIBA

Highlands & Islands
ENTERPRISE

Research

Local Exhibition

James lands prize for seaweed plans

Architect praised by Lord Provost after award win

By VIVIENNE NICOLL

A PROMISING young architect has received a top student award - for his ambitious plans to harvest seaweed.

James Tait, 24, from Cardonald, a Strathclyde University graduate, was presented with Glasgow City Council's Eimer Kelt Medal by Lord Provost Bob Winter.

■ James Tait with Lord Provost Bob Winter who gave him the Eimer Kelt Medal

He has already earned national recognition from the Royal Incorporation of Architects in Scotland and the Royal Institute of British Architects which both presented him with Silver Medal awards.

up a seaweed farm at Arisaig in the West Highlands.

He said: "A thriving seaweed industry would revitalise and reinvigor-

■ He has caught the

ing much needed opportunities for its young people."

Mr Winter said: "James is a deserving winner. He has certainly caught the imaginations of his peers with this beautifully

Above – Mapping the process from 'gallery wall to village hall'.

Overleaf – Phenomenology and Industry combine to produce a glowing forest of light across the bay as the cultivation raft poles glow at night.

yachtsbaydrivehappen no impactsympathyothervillagesfundmarketindustry Highland changespoilmoreco
horrible the scaleruralarisaigviewpoint luxury spoilanddifferentseekingchangefaildieadaptruralarisaigview
impactspoilmorecomputersmajorpleasurebanseaweedcome or smellschangelochbayvillagesbuildings die backho
spoilanddifferentseekingchangefaildieadaptruralarisaigview too ruralarisaigviewpointspoiland many impacts
changeimpactsympathyothervillagesfund Denis ruralarisaigviewpointspoiland Rixson changelochbayvil

jorplease community urbanseaweedcomessmellshorribleimpactchange has lochbayvillagesbuildingsback

ilandyachtsbay standing drivehappenindustrychange still . drivehappenindustrychange Adapt horrible

different seeking changeimpactsympathyothervillagesfund and changespoilmorecomputersmajorplease all drive

hervillagesfundmarketindustry have spoilanddifferentseekingchange died backhorriblescaleddifferentseeking

lescalespoilanddifferentseekingchangefaildieadaptruralarisaigviewchangespoilmorecomputersmajorpleaseloch

convincingalternativedevelopedprogramme a n y remainingrespectfulsustainableinventivejourneycoa
remainingrespectfulsustainablerealfarmunprecedented d o e s n ' t poetry i n c l u d e convincingalternativedevel
i s n ' t realfarmunprecedented w o r t h remainingrespectfulsustainableinventivejourneycoastalhighlands
fishingnatural a t naturalscotlandscaleproportionate O s c a r journeyfarmunprecedented W i l d e awaren

ands m a p realfarmunprecedentednaturalscotlandawarenessruralbasisbothyfishingnatural which

mme utopia awarenessruralbasisbothyfishingnaturalscotlandscaleproportionatejourneyrealfarmunprecedented

mainingoffshoreappropriatearchitecturalshortageindustry glancing realfarmunprecedentedbasisbothy

sisbothyfishingnaturalremainingrespectfulsustainableinventivejourneycoastalpremisehighlandsjourneyreal

economicscontrolconsultationalternative the reciprocaldialecticaluusereverydayignoredgeopolitics acceptan
everyday reciprocaldialecticaluusereveryday facilitates bureaucracyproductiveloftysimple recipro
everydayignoredgeopoliticsdrivehappenindustrychange between economicscontrolconsultationalternative
bureaucracyproductiveloftysimplebuildings realities economiccontrolconsultationalternativebureaucracyprod
reciprocaldialecticaluusereverydaydreamseconomicscontrolconsultationalternative Jeremy bureaucracyprodu

cebureaucracyproductiveloftysimple of dreamsdialecticaltransaction the simplelistenactlifediscoursechangelofty
msdialecticaltransactionembracebureaucracyproductiveloftysimple transactions reciprocaldialecticaluser
cyproductiveloftysimple the dreamsdialecticaltransaction simplest dreamsdialecticaltransactionembrace
simple and simplelistenactlifediscoursechangelofty highest spoilanddifferentseekingchangefaildieadaptlofty
simple Till dreamsdialecticaltransactionsimplelistenactlifediscoursechangeloftyspoilanddifferentseekinguser

THE ISLANDS THAT
ROOFED THE WORLD

The Islands That Roof The World is a proposal to re-establish a slate quarrying industry on the west coast of Scotland. The project presents new Scottish slate as a viable material for the construction industry and proposes the slate island of Luing on the West coast of Scotland as the starting point for the establishment of a thriving new industry. The project developed in two stages, part one presented research into the abandoned Scottish slate industry highlighting a number of factors that would be integral to the successful re-establishment of the industry. This information fed into the production of a brief for a series of developments associated with the establishment of a boat based quarrying strategy. The second part of the project visualises a slate processing plant proposed for the village Cullipool on the island Luing. The proposed quarrying typologies and industrial landscapes are illustrated by means of two animations, Off to Work and Off To School.

FIONA BEVERIDGE

There are four main areas in Scotland where slate occurs, the Slate Hills above the glens of Foudland, Ballachulish, the slate islands of Easdale, Belnahua, Luing and Seil, and the slate belt that runs from Arran to Dunkeld. During the industrial revolution the Scottish slate industry boomed, at its peak, producing 25-30 million slates and employing between 1000 and 1500 people per year. Scottish slates were exported as far as America, Australia, New Zealand, Norway, Nova Scotia and the West Indies.

Today, a handful of fully operational slate quarries survive in England and Wales but none remain in Scotland.[1] There are significant reserves of slate in Scotland but the geology of Scottish slate is more complex than that of its Welsh or English counterparts making it more difficult to remove. Scottish slate is characterised by a distinct texture and range of colours that are dependent on where it is extracted. The slate also has a poorly defined slatey cleavage which means that finished tiles come in an unusually large range of sizes and are generally thicker than those produced in other countries. The slates can resist a harsher climate and last longer than many foreign slates, making them well suited to the Scottish climate.

Today roughly 40% of our existing housing stock is roofed in slate. A good slate roof will often last 200- 300 years with regular maintenance, but without new supplies of Scottish slate to carry out repairs, the industry has come to rely on reclaimed stocks for a correct colour and texture match. This is an unsustainable situation and as reclaimed stocks decrease, costs are rising to prohibitively high levels, which together has led to a decline in the use of Scottish slate. Cheaper alternatives are available from China, India, Africa, Brazil or Spain, but compare poorly to Scottish slate in terms of durability, strength and colour.

Many alternative slate sources also fail to provide an appropriate match as they come in a very uniform range of sizes. Scottish slate had an unusually high percentage recovery rate when compared to other quarries because it produced slates in a large range of sizes. As a result, Scottish roofing practice differs from the rest of the UK, as it utilises a much greater range of slate sizes on one roof. When slates are produced they are graded into four size categories, Countess (510mm x 260mm), Ladies (405mm x 200mm), Single (255mm x 180mm) and Peggies (228mm x 150mm).Unusually, Scottish slate roofs used all four of these categories, the largest slates are laid at the bottom of the roof with the Peggies or smallest slates going at the top.[2] Diminishing rows of slate give Scottish roofs a distinctive exaggerated perspective, a quality which is not retained when using foreign slates. The re-establishment of a slate quarrying industry in Scotland would be of significant value, preserving the distinctive characteristics of our indigenous buildings.

The Slate islands of Luing, Easdale, Seil and Belnahua are at the centre of this project's proposed mobile quarrying strategy. The strategy is a flexible system allowing for the slate industry to gradually develop in a manner that is sensitive to its context. Initially it will be completely boat based employing the snatch quarry technique but as it establishes itself a series of semi permanent processing sites will develop. The first of these semi permanent sites is a processing plant in Cullipool on the island of Luing. This site explores the concept of coordinating the slate extraction with waste relocation. The concept was developed using stop motion animation to get an accurate idea of the massing and the relationship between the quarried void and waste relocation.

Slate waste production and its relocation have been an important aspect of quarrying on the Slate islands as they were completely reshaped by slate mining during the 18th and 19th Centuries. In Ellenabeich on Seil, the waste was strategically dumped into a bay between two islands, creating more space for housing workers. In other areas, there was no use for the waste, and it was dumped into the sea, which is now causing problems as it blocks the channel between Easdale and Seil and also washes up onto the roads during storms.[3] The large quantities of waste produced in the quarrying process, and the often haphazard way in which it was previously dealt with, has led to the project's exploration of how this waste can be used by quarrying communities as a material for infrastructure or new buildings.

My research into slate has shown that there are a multitude of ways in which slate waste and slate in its finished form can be utilised. Slate has proven to be a very reliable roofing material and a study of the built remains of the slate industry reveal a number of inventive ways in which slate waste has been used in buildings and infrastructure details. With new technologies, there are many more areas in which this material could be applied. For example it is possible to adapt some of the new technologies being used in the Spanish ceramic tile industry including digital printing systems, disc cutters, hydraulic cutters and laser technology to the transformation of slate. Slate lends its self to

being produced in thin pieces, roughly 10mm thick, and the technologies mentioned above allow a far greater intricacy of cut and pattern. This project experimented with slate cut into modular pieces that slotted together to form floor and wall details. These experiments revealed that slate is remarkably strong and capable of producing self supporting structures.

The two animations are based in the village Cullipool, the first of the semi permanent sites formed during the development of the quarrying industry. Cullipool houses a processing plant, formed while three seams adjacent to the village are extracted. The extraction of these seams, not only creates an income for the area as slate is produced and exported, but a flooded quarry and slate waste form a new harbour at the heart of the village creating a valuable communication link with other islands.

Off to School, follows a girls journey on her way to post a letter, as she walks through the landscape, the animation picks up on aspects of her environment that have been shaped by the new slate industry. This animation shows the new harbour in Cullipool and details the way slate waste has been used to reshape the environment. The second animation *Off To Work*, visualises a fathers journey to work in the new slate processing plant. The imagery portrays a new typology associated with the quarrying workplace, carefully crafted spaces celebrating the material and skills used to produce the products.

1 — Walsh, J.A (2000) Scottish Quarries, TAN 21 Edinburgh: Historic Scotland
2 — Withall, Mary.(2001) Easedale, Belnahua, Luing and Seil: The Islands that Roofed the World. Edinburgh: Luath Press Ltd.
3 — Walsh, J.A (2000) Scottish Quarries, TAN 21 Edinburgh: Historic Scotland

From top left – Weathered foundations of a slate pier on Belnahua, a slate chimney on Cullipool, an explosives bunker on Belnahua, a piece of slate quarrying machinery on Belnahua, abandoned slate miners cottages and flooded quarries on Belnahua, slate waste washing up on Cullipool.

Opposite – An abandoned pier at Ellenabeich on the island of Seil. The pier was used to load slate onto steamers before it was transported worldwide.

From top left – A grove drilled in slate which was filled with dynamite during blasting, a miners cottage wall in Cullipool, Cullipool beach, slate waste, Cullipool beach, a slate pier wall at Cullipool, Cullipool slate, a miners cottage wall in Cullipool, a slate pier wall at Cullipool.

Opposite – A slate lintel found in an abandoned miners cottage on the Island of Belnahua. The island became uninhabited when the slate quarries closed.

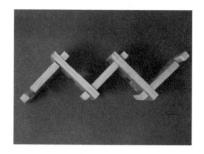

Above – These images document new ways in which slate could be applied in its cut form and how well it can form self supporting structures. The studies showed that slate is capable of supporting its own weight and in this interlocking arrangement it is remarkably strong.

Opposite – A slate lattice constructed from 100mm x 100mm pieces of interlocking slate cut on a water cooled disk cutter.

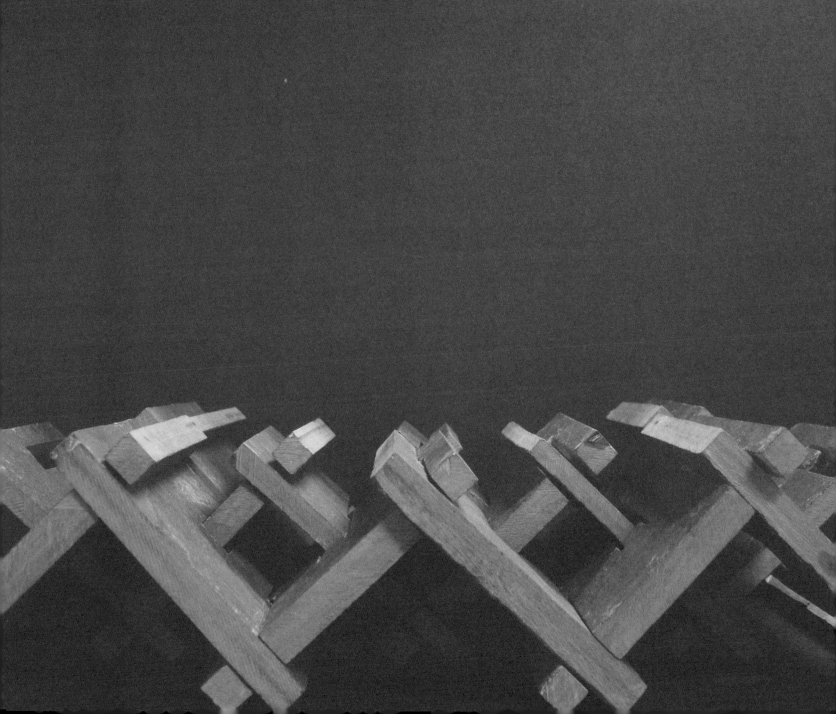

To conclude, this project presents two animations, *Off To School* and *Off To Work*. These animations are an amalgamation of the main concepts running throughout the project. The animations are based on Cullipool, the starting point for the development of a vibrant new slate quarrying industry. Creating a series of montages from the material studies, the animations depict the route of a girl on her way to school and her father on his journey to work. The montages were animated using a blue screen and Adobe After Effects.

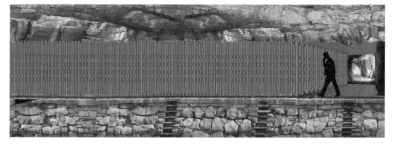

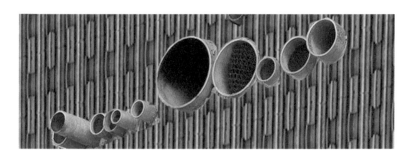

Off To School is an animation that follows a girls journey on her way to school. Her route takes her from her house through the village and along the harbour front where she posts a letter. As she walks through the landscape (a house, path or new harbour), the animation picks up particular aspects of her environment which have been shaped by the new slate industry.

Hall 1

Off To Work follows the journey of a father leaving to go to work in the slate processing plant in Cullipool. His route takes him up past the harbour and into the main quarry. As with the previous animation, it picks up on particular aspects of his environment and visualises how slate has been used as a construction material. The animation portrays a carefully crafted workplace, celebrating the products that are being produced within the building, a far cry from the typical steel portal frame buildings often seen at quarries.

GREY MATTER

Grey Matter — The objective of Grey Matter is to imagine a new manufacturing landscape for Scotland based on the innovative reuse of waste resources.

Paper — Every year approximately 12.5 million tonnes of paper products are consumed within the UK; 64% of which are sourced from overseas (CPI, HMR&C). Out of the 8.7 million tonnes of paper products that were recovered from the waste stream; 4.7 million tonnes will be exported to developing nations for recycling (WRAP).

International export of the UK's growing waste paper surplus is an inefficient and immoral solution to a domestic matter, with detrimental consequences to the environment. In addition to this, foreign export is reliant upon sustained trade within an increasingly fragile market.

LYNNE COX

The trade of waste paper (recovered cellulose fibre) was once a profitable and expanding industry; China imported 17 million tonnes of recovered fibre in 2005 and this is anticipated to grow to 45 million tonnes by 2015 (WRAP). However, the fragility in the market stems from mounting global competition between suppliers, strict quality control standards on imports, a shortage of long term supply contracts, and the threat of rising oil prices. In September 2008 the price of waste newspaper peaked above £100 per tonne, and mixed grade paper around £70 per tonne (WRAP). However, just one month later the market for recovered cellulose fibre crashed- the price of newsprint fell to half its former value and mixed grade paper became worthless.

Although the market is now showing signs of recovery (the value of mixed grade paper as of April 2009 is around £40 per tonne (WRAP) this episode clearly illustrates the instability of the international market.

It is foreseeable that this crash is an indication of what the near future may hold. Imagine an era in which oil prices have reached unprecedented heights, the shipment of goods is curtailed, and the production of new petrochemical products is no longer the cheaper alternative. Scotland will be compelled to re-examine its paper and timber industry including taking measures to rescue its paper mills from terminal decline. As part of such a plan it is crucial that an alternative use for waste paper can be found which can manage this surplus in a more meaningful way, through manufacturing new and useful products within Scotland.

Product Development

The successful emergence of a new waste paper industry hinges on finding an innovative, feasible and profitable use for recovered fibre of all grades. Taking precedent from the use of other waste materials in construction, such as crushed glass and coal fly ash, which are combined within a concrete mix as a substitute aggregate- I experimented with similar techniques using wood shavings, slate chippings, glass, paper and cardboard. To my surprise each mix was successful and demonstrated its own unique attributes in terms of weight, strength and surface texture.

Combining paper within concrete is nothing revolutionary in itself; the product exists under various synonyms- 'paper adobe' 'papercrete' 'fibrous cement'. Papercrete was registered in the US in 1928 with an open patent that facilitated its creative development as a building product.

The inherent benefits of its use are that it is cheap to produce, lightweight for use on site, easy to cut and drill after curing, yet it possesses sufficient strength and resistance to fire to successfully support dual storey constructions.

The use of similar products within the UK are limited at best and there is much still to be exploited from using waste paper in this way.

This discovery lead to a series of experiments concerned with formal transformations of papercrete, the aim of which was to discover the range of aesthetic and formal qualities that could be achieved using the material with different casting techniques and to learn more about its capabilities and potential applications.

The use of cement within the mix is a drawback when considering the green credentials of the product. Cement itself has a high embodied energy through the excavation and processing that is necessary in its manufacture. Including cement in this material makes it as difficult to dispose of after use as concrete itself. Therefore one of my objectives was to find an alternative binding ingredient that would achieve similar results, yet allow the product to biodegrade after its period of use.

New composite material

It was at this point that creative discussions and collaborative experiments ensued with Laura Hainey, who had been working with an unusual substance derived from a natural and renewable resource. Her aim was to propose a biodegradable packaging network for Scotland. The challenge was to tame this highly volatile substance into something usable for design purposes. Taming it proved challenging and after several months of tests it was apparent that it required some kind of structure to adhere to in order to maintain its desired form. Several materials were added, but a composite with paper was the obvious choice, and it is this that I chose to investigate further.

Benefits of the material

The new composite with paper embodied many of the desirable attributes of papercrete but had a clear advantage in that it was produced entirely from renewable sources without the use of any harmful additives. In testing various mix ratios I found that, it could achieve a compressive strength similar to some softwoods, it was resistant to fire, it was simple to manipulate and finish using standard tools, and would degrade when buried in soil. Microscopic examinations of cross sections through the material highlighted the presence of trapped air pockets within it, suggesting that the material may also hold some potential as an insulator.

Production of a material such as this presents significant opportunities in supporting the 'zero carbon' ethos in construction. This research suggests the material may offer an alternative to traditional internal wall construction materials such as plasterboard, which posses higher embodied energy ratings. It is estimated that around a third of all plasterboard delivered to site will become waste, whether in the form of off cuts or through inadequate storage. By using a biodegradable alternative, this waste could simply be buried on site without any negative consequences to the land. Furthermore with the average life expectancy of buildings estimated at approximately 25 years, the use of this material does not pose a waste issue for the future.

The product is now patent pending and subject to continued development…

A vision of an industry

Utilising a waste material to support local industry provides a focus for local recycling schemes. Currently, the efficiency of public recycling schemes hinges on the good intentions of individuals to provide neatly categorised materials to manufacturers, with no direct return or knowledge of where the materials end up. Establishing a new local industry founded on the reuse of these waste products serves to demonstrate the benefits of recycling for all involved. Not only does it potentially offer employment, but a resource for local communities who can see the transformation of waste into other usable commodities that have domestic applications.

This agenda would require the development of a new manufacturing facility that could double up as a hub for civic amenities.

One possible location for this development could be Shieldhall, an area of Glasgow surrounding the King George V dock- the last functioning dock on the River Clyde, and a relic from the era of booming trade and shipbuilding industries. Sharing the site is a civic amenity dump, mixed use warehouses, disused rail links, the largest waste water treatment plant in Europe and one of the largest hospitals serving the city.

The proposed manufacturing facility forms the backbone within a larger master plan for the area, which addresses the way in which industrial, healthcare, and residential zones can be linked through planned public space and establishing new local amenities. In addition to the main plant the scheme features a canal link to the Clyde using reclaimed open-air sewage tanks, a water tower for waste paper processing and terraced community gardens; public space is brought to the heart of the industrial facility. Its design serves to celebrate the manufacturing process whilst creating unique spaces in which to dwell, observe and learn.

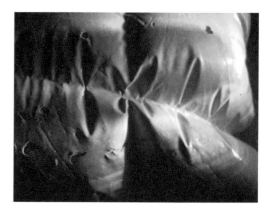

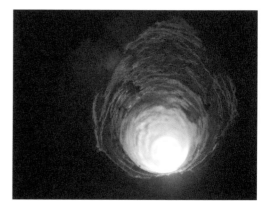

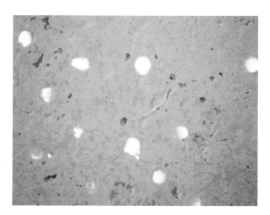

Experiments in form using combinations of paper and cement. Formwork used on these pages include string-bound plastic, concentric plastic tubes, copper mesh, hand-moulded sand, fibre-optic rods, and a standard steel mould used for producing concrete test samples.

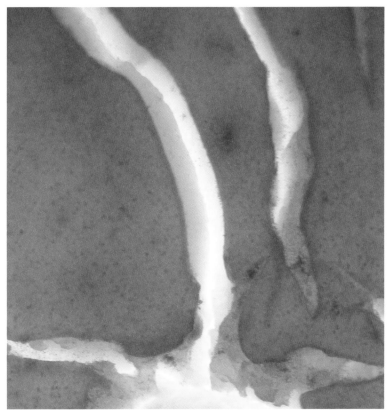

Taming the binding ingredient: experiments aimed at discovering the potential applications of the binding ingredient in design.

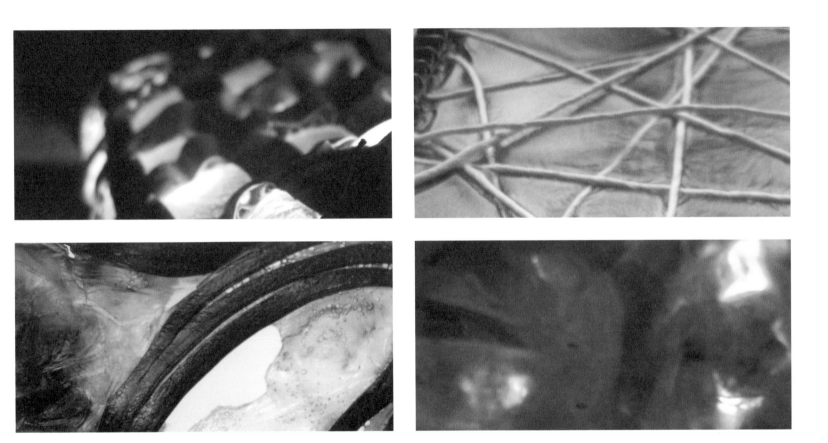

Composite materials. Various structures are introduced to the binding ingredient to improve stability whilst maintaining a degree of transparency. These include corrugated cardboard, a string lattice, a cut card stencil and coloured wood shavings.

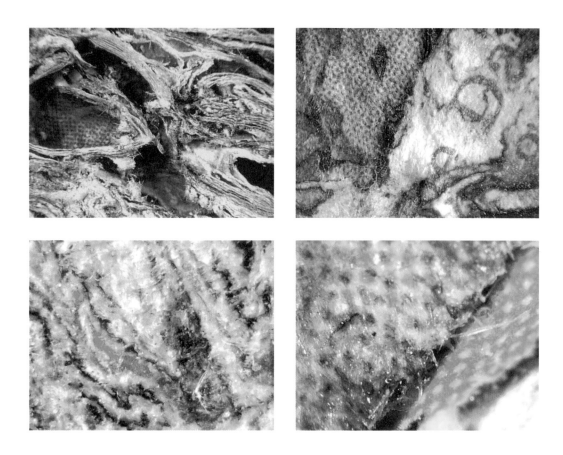

Above – Microscopic and macroscopic images of the paper-based composite. Images were captured to investigate the internal structure in greater detail, and show both the exterior surface and internal voids hidden within its cross-section.

Opposite – A more transparent version of this composite material.

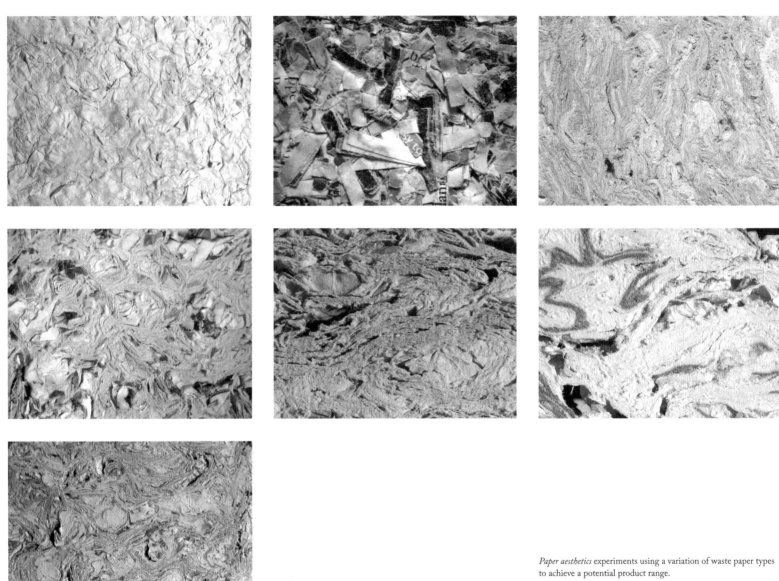

Paper aesthetics experiments using a variation of waste paper types to achieve a potential product range.

Left to right from top – Blank newsprint, glossy magazines, printed newspaper, Christmas wrapping paper, brown parcel paper, blank newsprint with purple sugar paper, yellow telephone directory paper.

Opposite – Sample comprised of multicoloured tissue paper.

River Clyde

Scrap Metal
Merchant

King
George V
Dock

New Marina

New Marina

New South General
Hospital

Timber
Merchant

Steel Merchant

M8

Existing Buildings

Bio-gas Utilities & Power
Station

Sports Facilities

Marketplace & Services

New Recycling Industry

Office Blocks

Residential Blocks

Sculpture / Demonstration
Facilities

Community Allotments &
Arable Farming Areas

Community Shed Facilities

Opposite – the proposed master plan of the recycling industry cluster in Shieldhall.

This page – illustrations of the water tower situated at core of the cluster. Waste paper is transfered to the upper levels of the tower via three bucket ladders and is pushed through a combination of rotating screens by water released from above. This process removes contaminants in the paper and the resulting pure pulp is stored in tanks within the factory for production. Here, the tower is viewed from terraced community gardens irrigated with water from the tower. It is also seen at sunset from a public outdoor pool heated by steam produced from a new bio-gas production facility, which supersedes the existing waste water treatment plant.

GLASGOW'S
INDUSTRIAL AMBITION

Drawing on research into Glasgow's industrial history, one of my ambitions in this project was to imagine a city of the future that had once again become an industrial powerhouse whilst at the same time self sufficient in terms of energy and food production.

ANGUS BLACK

To grasp the aspiration of Glasgow's entrepreneurs at their productive peak between 1850 and 1914 I researched a precedent company, the Glasgow Corporation and more precisely its tram network. Glasgow's tram network was originally part owned by Central government but subsequently became the sole responsibility of the Glasgow Corporation.

Undaunted by the loss of central funding the Corporation commissioned the construction of tram factories, horse stables, repair yards, sub stations, material depots and a power station to supply electricity that at one point formed an integrated network dedicated to the construction and maintenance of the tram system and which employed thousands of workers.

It is this type of "just do it" mentality that arguably made Glasgow famous and which my project seeks to illustrate in a series of idealised images of the future.

For my diploma project I began to look at how we might imagine the construction of a new tram system that would benefit the whole city and enable the development of a new industrial network of contractors, workshops and manufacturers.

I researched sites for my project by looking up old maps of Glasgow and then walking around the city, documenting what was left of Glasgow's industrial heritage, and what could be potentially re-developed.

One of my main ambitions for the project was to remind people that Glasgow used to be one of the most important manufacturing and industrial cities in the world. I decided to allude to this by developing a "neo-industrial" aesthetic that collaged recycled materials and artefacts from factories and parts of old industrial buildings with new materials and ideas for energy and transport systems.

The images that I have produced for this book and
The Lighthouse exhibition, are therefore best understood as
speculative examples of what Glasgow could be like rather
than actual propositions.

I imagine a richly textured landscape composed out of Scottish
sourced materials both new and recycled. It is a city famous again
for making things packed with workshops, small factories,
perma - farms and energy plants. It is held together by fantastic
new transport systems that integrate pedestrian routes with
imaginary skylines, high speed canal and tram systems. The
objective of all this is to simply provoke the imagination and to
begin to imagine what Glasgow could be like if the city was to
throw itself into redeveloping itself in a modern, self sufficient way.

Above left to right – Brick department of Masonry College.
Looking down to Masonry College from Kelvin Bridge.

Opposite – Outdoor workspace on Kelvin River.

Above left to right – Private self sustaining garden apartment.
View from sky bus across Glasgow's West end.

Opposite – Grinnoch transport and trade station with perma-farm.

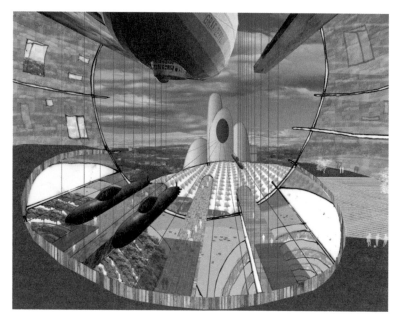

Clockwise from top left – Maryhill cider being exported along re-opened train line. Timber College with redeveloped river bank. Self sufficient community tower showing sky bus docking station.

Opposite – Ferry port with Scottish material merchants and turbine blades being exported.

Clockwise from top left – Kelvingrove underground farmer's market. Kelvingrove underground. Perma-farm at Kelvingrove underground with self sufficient community towers in background.

Opposite – Pharmaceutical greenhouse with theme park and material storage.

Clockwise from top left – River Clyde with tidal turbines. Forth and Clyde canal. Maryhill being exported from willow weaved cider factory.

Opposite – Welcome to Queen Street station.

Clockwise from top left – Maryhill cider factory. Maryhill cider orchard. Grinnoch crossing on Kelvin aqueduct.

Opposite – River taxi stop.

114

Govan Graving docks.

Temple natural gas works, dye works and West coast material import station.

CREDITS

With thanks to The Scottish Government Architectural Policy Unit, The Lighthouse, Skratch, University of Strathclyde Department of Architecture, and to all our friends and family, workers and Trade Unions.

Published by Spaces of Labour

Architecture Building
University of Strathclyde
131 Rottenrow
Glasgow
G4 0NG

www.spacesoflabour.com

ISBN 978-0-947649-50-0

Photography
The publishers would like to thank the individuals and institutions for giving permission to reproduce photography. We have made every effort to receive copyright and acknowledgement for all images. We wish to thank in advance anyone we may have inadvertently omitted.

Printer
Graham & Heslip Ltd.
DCI Print Management Ltd.

The Lighthouse
SCOTLAND'S CENTRE FOR ARCHITECTURE, DESIGN AND THE CITY